Wood and Other Materials

Contents

Materials 2

Wood 4

Glass 6

Metal 8

Plastic 10

More Than One Material 12

Materials Chart and Answers 14

Index 16

Rigby

Materials

There are lots of different materials.

Wood

building blocks

baseball bat

table and chairs

house

Lots of things are made of wood.

4

Which things are made of wood?

Glass

marbles

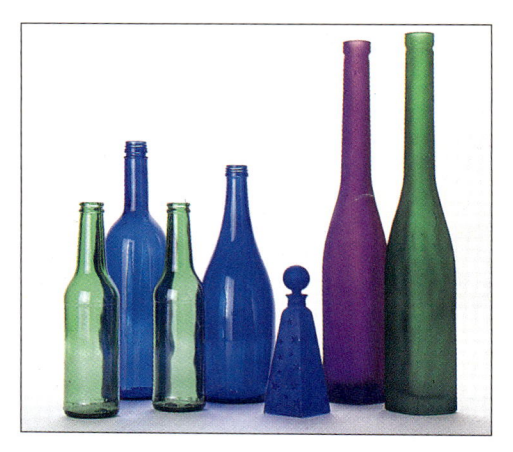

bottles

windows

Lots of things are made of glass.

Which things are made of glass?

Metal

money

saxophone

pots and pans

bridge

Which things are made of metal?

Plastic

buckets

bottles and bags

toys

raincoat

Lots of things are made of plastic.

Which things are made of plastic?

More Than One Material

glass

wood

Some things are made of more than one material.

metal

plastic

| Wood | Glass |

| Metal | Plastic |

a
b
c
d
e
f
g
h
i
j
k
l
m
n
o
p
q
r
s
t
u
v
w
x
y
z

16

Index

glass 6–7, 12, 14

metal 8–9, 13, 15

plastic 10–11, 13, 15

wood 4–5, 12, 14